Make an Egg Box Crab

Written by Becky Dickinson

Crabs can live on land and in the sea.

Rock pools can have crabs in them.

This crab is made from an egg box.

To make a crab, you will need:

egg box

paint and brush

glue

stick on eyes

fuzzy legs

Now we can make an egg box crab!

1. Get an adult to cut up the egg box.

2. Paint the crab with a bright colour.

3. Stick on the eyes and fuzzy legs.

glue

4. Bend the front legs to make claws.

Look at all the egg box animals!
The fish has fins.